James Madison
and the Making of the United States

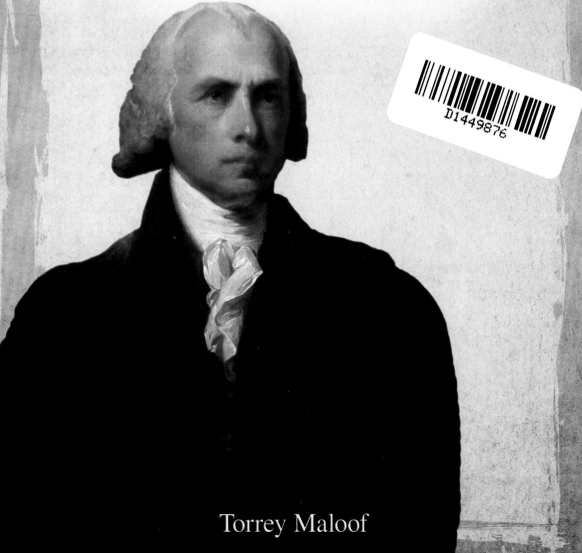

Torrey Maloof

Consultants

Vanessa Ann Gunther, Ph.D.
Department of History
Chapman University

Nicholas Baker, Ed.D.
Supervisor of Curriculum and Instruction
Colonial School District, DE

Katie Blomquist, Ed.S.
Fairfax County Public Schools

Publishing Credits

Rachelle Cracchiolo, M.S.Ed., *Publisher*
Conni Medina, M.A.Ed., *Managing Editor*
Emily R. Smith, M.A.Ed., *Series Developer*
Diana Kenney, M.A.Ed., NBCT, *Content Director*
Courtney Patterson, *Senior Graphic Designer*
Lynette Ordoñez, *Editor*

Image Credits: Cover and p. 4 NARA [1667751]; cover and p. 1 World History Archive/Alamy Stock Photo; p. 2 Steve Heap/Shutterstock.com; pp.5 (back), 9, 13, 21, 25 (top) North Wind Picture Archives; p. 5 National Numismatic Collection at the Smithsonian Institution; p. 6 (top) MPI/Getty Images, (bottom) DeAgostini/Getty Images; p. 7 (top) New York Public Library Digital Collections, (bottom) Pete Spiro/Shutterstock.com; p. 8 LOC [LC-DIG-ppmsc-08560]; p. 10 Kean Collection/Archive Photos/Getty Images; pp. 11, 23, 28 Granger, NYC; p. 17, 20 (middle) Sarin Images/Granger, NYC; p. 11 (left) GraphicaArtis/Bridgeman Images, (right) GraphicaArtis/Bridgeman Images, (top) Courtesy of the Historical Society of Pennsylvania Collection, Atwater Kent Museum of Philadelphia; p. 12 LOC [LC-USZ62-59464]; p. 14 U.S. Government/Public Domain; p. 15 LOC [Jefferson.21562v1.1]; p. 18 (front) LOC [LC-USZ62-68175]; pp. 18-19 LOC [LC-DIG-highsm-13867]; p. 20 (top) Natural Earth and Portland State University/Wikimedia Commons, (bottom) Library of Virginia; p. 21 (top) U.S. Naval History and Heritage Command, (bottom) LOC [LC-USZC4-6235]; pp. 22, 32 GraphicaArtis/Bridgeman Images; p. 24 Universal History Archive/UIG via Getty Images; p. 25 (bottom) LOC [LC-DIG-ppmsca-23756]; p. 26 (left) Steve Heap/Shutterstock.com, (right) LOC [LC-HS503-4621]; p. 29 LOC [bdsdcc n001001]; back cover MPI/Getty Images; all other images from iStock and/or Shutterstock.

Library of Congress Cataloging-in-Publication Data

Names: Maloof, Torrey, author.
Title: James Madison and the making of the United States / Torrey Maloof.
Description: Huntington Beach, CA : Teacher Created Materials, Inc., 2017. |
  Includes index.
Identifiers: LCCN 2016034139 (print) | LCCN 2016038168 (ebook) | ISBN
  9781493837953 (pbk.) | ISBN 9781480757608 (eBook)
Subjects: LCSH: Madison, James, 1751-1836--Juvenile literature. |
  Presidents--United States--Biography--Juvenile literature.
Classification: LCC E342 .M27 2017 (print) | LCC E342 (ebook) | DDC
  973.5/1092 [B] --dc23
LC record available at https://lccn.loc.gov/2016034139

Table of Contents

Create, Expand, Preserve 4

Small but Smart 6

Starting a Career 8

Creating the Constitution 12

A Close Friendship 18

Mr. Madison's War 22

Last Man Standing 26

Fix It! 28

Glossary 30

Index 31

Your Turn! 32

Create, Expand, Preserve

You may know him as the Father of the **Constitution**. But, did you know he did not think of himself as such? In fact, James Madison greatly disliked being called that. He famously stated that the document was not the work of his "single brain." Rather, it was "the work of many heads and many hands."

Madison was being humble with these words. His role in the history of the United States was both vast and vital. His impressive **résumé** (REH-zuh-may) speaks for itself. Madison helped create the U.S. government. Then, he helped expand the country's borders. Later, he helped preserve the nation during a war with Great Britain.

Madison was a member of Congress. He served as secretary of state. And he was the fourth president. Madison was an excellent writer, a deep thinker, and a problem solver. He loved his country, and it showed. During his life, he did what he could to expand and preserve the nation.

the U.S. Constitution

James Madison

$5,000 BILL

★★★★★★★

Yes, you read that right. Before World War II, the treasury made large currency bills. James Madison's face was on the $5,000 bill. There were also $500, $1,000, $10,000, and $100,000 bills.

Small but Smart

James Madison Jr. was born on March 16, 1751. He was the first of 12 children. His family was wealthy. They owned a large plantation called Mount Pleasant in the colony of Virginia. It was later named Montpelier (mont-PEEL-yer).

As a young child, Madison was small and sickly. He had stomach troubles. Doctors believed he had problems with his liver. He also suffered from violent seizures. Because of his ill health, Madison spent most of his days inside. He passed the time by reading. Madison had read every book in his father's library by the age of 11.

a young James Madison

James Madison's home in Montpelier

At this time, Madison was sent to boarding school. Before that, he had been tutored at home. While at school, Madison studied math, history, and geography. He also learned Greek, Latin, and French. He was a gifted student. At the age of 16, he returned home and was tutored for two more years.

By the age of 18, Madison was just over five feet tall. He barely weighed 100 pounds. He was small for his age, and still quite sickly, but he did not let that stop him. He was off to college!

College of New Jersey

COLLEGE YEARS ★ ★

Madison attended the College of New Jersey. Today, it is known as Princeton University. It took Madison only two years to finish his studies there.

present-day Princeton University

Starting a Career

After college, Madison was a bit lost. He was unsure of what he wanted to do with his life. Things were changing quickly in the world around him. There was talk of the colonies breaking free from Great Britain. Colonists were tired of all the taxes. They wanted representation in **Parliament**. They needed to be treated fairly. Madison thought independence was a good idea. He felt that colonists should have more control over their lives. Madison wanted to help play a role in gaining independence. So, he chose a life of public service. He was going to work in the government.

the British Houses of Parliament in London

Madison's first job was in Virginia. He was elected to the Committee of Safety. This group oversaw the local **militia** (mi-LISH-uh). It was their job to make sure that people were ready for war and that they supported Virginia, not Great Britain. Tensions were high between the British and the colonists. A war could start at any time!

a colonial militia

TOO WEAK TO SERVE

Madison joined the militia he helped form. However, he was too weak to keep up with the drills. He fainted on the first day!

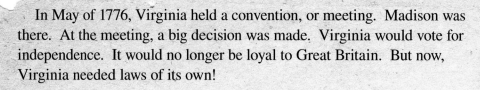

In May of 1776, Virginia held a convention, or meeting. Madison was there. At the meeting, a big decision was made. Virginia would vote for independence. It would no longer be loyal to Great Britain. But now, Virginia needed laws of its own!

More meetings were held. This time, the goal was to create a constitution. Madison listened closely at the meetings. He loved learning how government worked. He found it all very interesting. In a few months time, Virginia had its own constitution.

Madison wanted a bigger role in government. So in 1777, he ran for a seat in the state assembly. But, he lost. It was not really a fair fight. His **opponent** gave out free whiskey on the day of the election! However, Madison was chosen for another role. He was asked to join the Virginia Council of State. This was a group of eight men who helped the governor make decisions. It was a good start to a budding career.

THE AMERICAN REVOLUTION

★★★★★

Two months after Virginia decided to break free from Great Britain, the colonies declared independence. General George Washington led the Continental Army to victory in 1781. A peace treaty was signed two years later. The United States of America was born.

The 13 colonies agree to declare independence shortly after Virginia decided to do so.

THE VIRGINIA DECLARATION OF RIGHTS

This section from the Virginia Constitution of 1776 was written by George Mason.

A FRIENDSHIP IS FORMED

★★★★

Madison met Thomas Jefferson in 1776. The two had a lot in common. Jefferson was impressed by Madison's knowledge and love of politics. They soon became close friends.

Creating the Constitution

In 1779, Madison took a big leap in his political career. He was elected to the **Continental Congress**. At just 28 years old, he was the youngest **delegate** there. At that time, Congress was working on a plan. They needed to form a **federal** government. They wrote the Articles of Confederation. This was the young nation's first set of laws. People were fearful of having a strong central government. So, the Articles left the state governments intact. Each state had its own set of laws. Congress could not collect taxes from the states. Nor could they raise an army. Madison did not agree with the plan. He knew it had problems. But, the plan was passed in 1781.

As time went on, more people saw flaws in the Articles. These people wanted changes made. They hoped to strengthen the federal government. They worried the country would fall apart if they did not.

ARTICLES
OF
CONFEDERATION
AND
PERPETUAL UNION
BETWEEN THE
STATES
OF
w-Hampshire   chusetts-Bay,

A Massachusetts militia battles protesters during Shays's Rebellion.

SHAYS'S REBELLION

★★★★★★★

From 1786 to 1787, a man named Daniel Shays led farmers in a series of protests. He said he would start a war because farmers couldn't pay their debts. They wanted the government to help them pay, but it couldn't. Congress had no army. It had no power to stop the rebellion. People now understood why the government needed to change.

George Washington leads a meeting in 1787 to revise the Articles of Confederation.

Madison attended a meeting in Philadelphia in 1787. This meeting came to be known as the Constitutional Convention. Leaders from all the states except Rhode Island were there. They were there to discuss ways to improve the Articles.

Virginia sent several men to the convention. Madison was one of them. Before the meeting, he did his homework. Madison researched political **philosophies**. He read many books. He studied governments from all over the world. He took note of what had worked in the past. He thought about why other systems had not worked. Then, Madison came up with a plan.

The Virginia Plan called for a larger central government. It had to be stronger than the states. The plan said a state's population should determine the number of delegates it would have in Congress. And it called for a three-part system. Each part, or branch, would check and balance the power of the others. It was a solid plan. But now, Madison had to convince the leaders to accept it. He worked hard. He gave speeches. He **compromised**. In the end, the leaders agreed! They created the Constitution.

The U.S. Constitution is signed in 1787.

The Constitution explains how power in the U.S. government is shared among three branches.

Legislative Branch

Judicial Branch

Executive Branch

THE FEDERALIST PAPERS

★★★

Once the Constitution was approved, citizens had to vote for it before it could become law. James Madison, Alexander Hamilton, and John Jay wrote newspaper articles known as the Federalist Papers to explain the Constitution to the American people.

For Mr Church from her sister Elizabeth Hamilton

THE

FEDERALIST:

A COLLECTION

OF

ESSAYS,

WRITTEN IN FAVOUR OF THE

NEW CONSTITUTION,

AS AGREED UPON BY THE FEDERAL CONVENTION, SEPTEMBER 17, 1787.

IN TWO VOLUMES.

VOL. I.

NEW-YORK:

PRINTED AND

In 1788, the Constitution was **ratified**, or approved. That same year, Madison won a seat in the House of Representatives. It was not long before Madison was a leader in Congress. He was still shy and quiet, but many people respected him. They knew he had great ideas.

Madison served in Congress until 1797. During that time, he helped form the national court system. This system decides whether people have broken the law. He also proposed different departments to help the president. They would deal with issues such as finance and war. They would give advice to the president and help him make decisions.

Madison's major triumph while in Congress was the Bill of Rights. This is a list of additions to the Constitution. It promises and protects the basic rights of the citizens. Madison pushed for the Bill of Rights to be added. He also wrote many of them! They were based on George Mason's Declaration of Rights.

The Supreme Court is the highest court in the national court system.

U.S. Constitution

President Washington's cabinet members led the departments that Madison had suggested.

A Close Friendship

During his final years in Congress, Madison worked hard. But he also found some time for himself. In 1794, he met the lovely and lively Dolley Payne Todd. She was a **widow**. The pair appeared to be exact opposites. She was fun and outgoing. He was serious and shy. Yet the two became smitten with each other. In just a few months, they married.

DOLLEY'S EARLY LIFE

Dolley Payne was born a Quaker in 1768. In 1790, she married a lawyer named John Todd Jr. They had two sons. In 1793, Dolley's husband and youngest son died of yellow fever.

Dolley Madison

18

In 1797, George Washington left office. He had served two **terms**. John Adams became the new president. That year, Madison decided he would retire, too. He was tired. He wanted a change. He returned home to Virginia with his wife, though he still took part in state government from time to time.

Over the next few years, the couple remodeled the family home. Dolley charmed guests in her new house. Madison relished the calmness of life on the farm. The couple was content. Life was good at Montpelier. But in 1801, everything changed. Madison's close friend, Thomas Jefferson, became president. He had a big question for Madison.

Madison's home in Virginia

James Madison

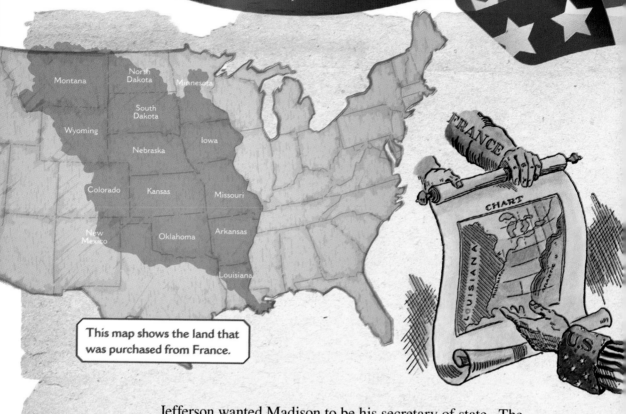

This map shows the land that was purchased from France.

Jefferson wanted Madison to be his secretary of state. The two men had been close friends for more than 20 years. Madison could not refuse. He accepted the offer. He and Dolley moved to Washington, DC.

Madison's new job was not easy. He was in charge of foreign affairs. This meant he worked with other countries. He advised the president. He told him what was happening in the world.

MARBURY VS. MADISON

Chief Justice John Marshall

As John Adams left office, he appointed several judges. When Jefferson took over, he didn't want those men to be judges. So, he asked Madison not to deliver the new judges' papers to appoint them. The issue went to the Supreme Court. The Court overruled Jefferson's wish. This case helped establish the Supreme Court as equal to the other two branches of government.

20

The British attack an American ship in 1807.

One of Madison's first tasks involved France. The United States wanted to purchase the Port of New Orleans from France. In 1803, a deal was made. Instead of selling just the port, France sold the whole Louisiana Territory for $15 million. Just like that, the nation almost doubled in size!

Madison also had to deal with problems at sea. Great Britain and France were trying to restrict American trade. The British started attacking U.S. ships. In 1807, Madison and Jefferson brought the Embargo Act to Congress. It said the United States could not ship goods to Europe anymore. The act passed, but it did not work. The United States lost money. Soon, Congress ended the act.

This 1808 political cartoon shows Americans complaining to Jefferson about the Embargo Act.

WHY IT FAILED

★★★★★★★★

The Embargo Act stopped trade with Europe. But, European countries continued to trade amongst themselves. They did not need the United States' goods like Madison and Jefferson hoped. Since the United States had no one to trade with, businesses started to fail.

Mr. Madison's War

Thomas Jefferson's second term as president had come to an end. He hoped his good friend James Madison would **succeed** him. He did! He won the election. Madison became president in 1809. His inauguration was in March. It was then that he gave a short speech. He said he wanted to "cherish peace." But soon, war was looming on the horizon.

During this time, the British were after American ships. They took cargo and abducted sailors. It hurt American trade. These problems plagued Madison during his first two years in office. He wanted to avoid going to war with Great Britain. But some congressmen spoke out in favor of it. They were called War Hawks. Under mounting pressure, Madison called Congress together to discuss the issue. In June of 1812, Congress declared war on Great Britain. This conflict became known as the War of 1812.

The war did not go well for the United States at first. Britain had a better army and navy. They put a naval **blockade** on the United States. British ships crowded the American coast. Goods could not leave the country. Nor could they be **imported**. Americans suffered as a result.

James Madison's presidential portrait

The USS *Constitution* defeats the British ship, HMS *Guerriere*, during the War of 1812.

Many were not happy with Madison during this period. They started calling the war, "Mr. Madison's War." This was a bad time for Madison. He was ill and his first term was coming to an end. Yet, Madison refused to give up. He was reelected in 1812. But the war continued.

In the summer of 1814, the British invaded Washington, DC. They smashed and plundered the city. They set fire to buildings, including the Capitol. Then, they headed for the President's House. They went from room to room stealing what they wanted and trashing the rest. Before they left, they set fire to the house. Madison was not at home at the time. Dolley fled just before the British arrived.

Soon, the United States started to win battles on land and at sea. A victory no longer seemed impossible. By this time, the British were tired of fighting. Americans were, too. Madison sent representatives to begin peace talks. A peace treaty was signed in December of 1814.

The United States defeats Great Britain at the Battle of New Orleans.

DOLLEY HELPS SAVE GEORGE ★★

Before fleeing the President's House, Dolley grabbed a copy of the Declaration of Independence. She saved silverware, books, and more. She also instructed servants and an enslaved man named Paul Jennings to save a famous portrait of George Washington.

THE WHITE HOUSE ★★★

Before it was set on fire, the house in which the president lived was called the President's House. When it was rebuilt, it was painted white. After that, it has been known as the White House.

25

Last Man Standing

After the war, Madison was thought of as a hero. He held firm in his beliefs. He fought the war fiercely. He kept the nation together and made it stronger.

Madison's second term came to an end in 1817. He was 66 years old. He and Dolley returned to Montpelier. He was ready for a quiet life on his farm.

One day, Thomas Jefferson came to visit. He needed Madison's help again. He wanted his old friend to work with him to start a university. Madison agreed. They helped create the University of Virginia.

statue of James Madison in Harrisonburg, Virginia

University of Virginia

In 1836, Madison was 85 years old. He was the last of the Founding Fathers still alive. He was frail and weak. He could no longer write or walk. On June 28, he passed away. He would be remembered as the small man with big ideas. He helped form a government, write a constitution, and keep a nation together. It seems fitting that, while he was the first Founding Father to arrive at the Constitutional Convention, he was the last to leave Earth.

HELPING FUTURE LEADERS ★★

Madison asked Dolley to help him edit and copy his papers from the Constitutional Convention. He could barely hold a pen due to his **rheumatism** (ROO-muh-tiz-uhm). But he hoped his notes would be useful to future leaders.

James Madison, age 82

Fix It!

James Madison was a problem solver. He was one of the men who understood the Articles of Confederation were not working well. He saw a problem and came up with new ideas to fix it.

Think of a problem at your home or school. How do you think this problem could be solved? Write a plan to solve the problem. Share your ideas with your family or classmates. Then, put your plan into action.

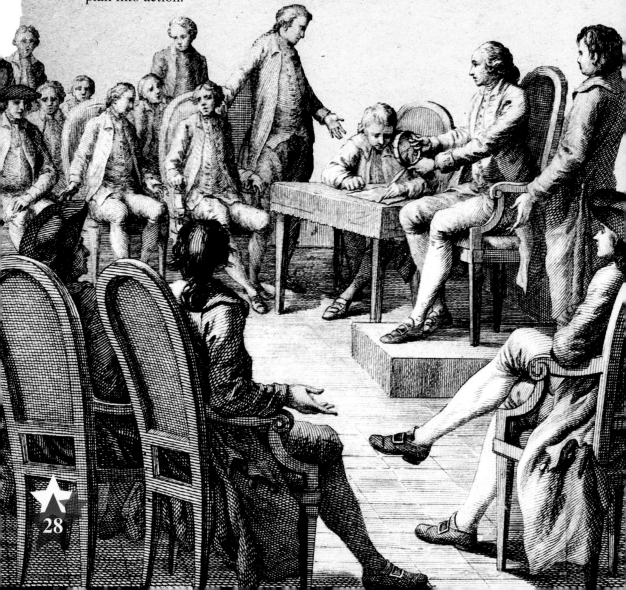

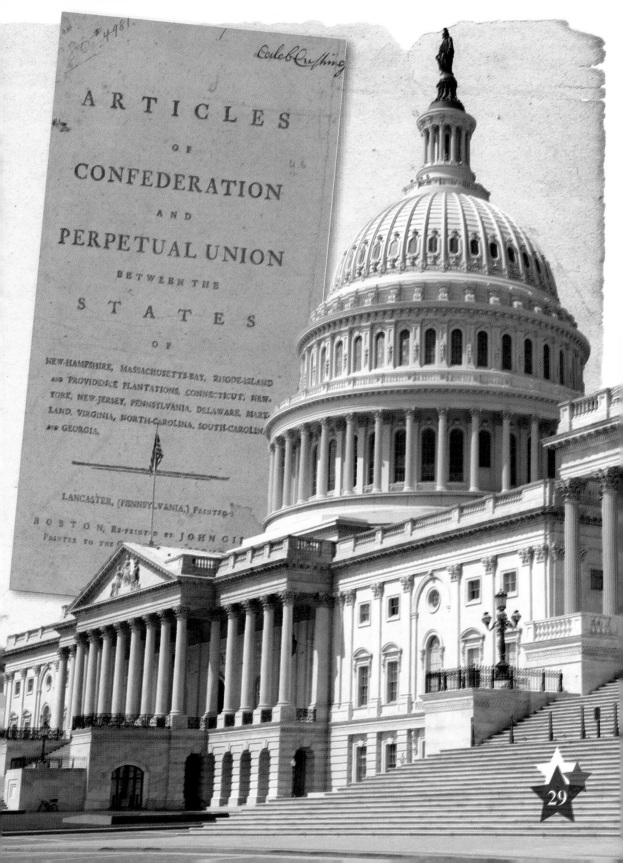

Glossary

blockade—an act of war in which ships are used to stop people and supplies from entering or leaving a country

compromised—gave up something that you wanted in order to reach an agreement

constitution—a system of beliefs, laws, and principles by which a country or state is governed

Continental Congress—government meetings of the colonists in America

delegate—a person chosen to speak for one of the colonies at the Continental Congress

federal—relating to the main government of the United States

imported—brought goods into a country from another country

militia—regular citizens trained in military combat and willing to fight and defend their country

opponent—a person that is competing against another person

Parliament—the supreme legislative body of Great Britain

philosophies— studies of ideas about knowledge, truth, and the meaning of life

ratified—made official by signing or voting

résumé—a short document that describes a person's work history and education

rheumatism—a disease that causes painful swelling of the muscles and joints

succeed—to come after someone or something in a series

terms—the length of time a person is in political office

widow—someone whose spouse has passed away

Index

Adams, John, 19–20

Articles of Confederation, 12–14, 28–29

Bill of Rights, 16

Constitution, 4, 12, 14–17

Constitutional Convention, 14, 27

Continental Congress, 12

Embargo Act, 21

Federalist Papers, 15

France, 20–21

Great Britain, 4, 8–10, 21–22, 24

Hamilton, Alexander, 15

Jay, John, 15

Jefferson, Thomas, 11, 19–22, 26, 32

Madison, Dolley, 18–20, 24–27

Montpelier, 6, 19, 26

Shays's Rebellion, 13

Todd, John, Jr., 18

University of Virginia, 26

Virginia, 6, 9–11, 14, 19, 26

Virginia Plan, 14

War of 1812, 22–24

Washington, DC, 20, 24

Washington, George, 10, 13, 17, 19, 25

Your Turn!

A Political Conversation

Thomas Jefferson and James Madison were good friends. Jefferson asked Madison for many favors over the years. He asked Madison to serve as his secretary of state. He also wanted Madison to help start a university. These are big tasks! Write a script that outlines a conversation Jefferson and Madison might have had when discussing one of these opportunities.

THE TUNISIAN AWAKENING

K. A. HUSSEIN

THE TUNISIAN AWAKENING
written and illustrated by Khalid A. Hussein

Copyright © 2011 by Khalid Hussein

www.khalidhussein.com
khalidiyya@gmail.com

First Edition

ISBN-13: 9748-1477433645
ISBN-10: 1477433643

Printed in the United States of America.

This book is dedicated to Muhammad Bouazizi and all the Arab people who are living and dying for change, as well as anyone across the globe who continues to strive for and believe in justice and freedom.

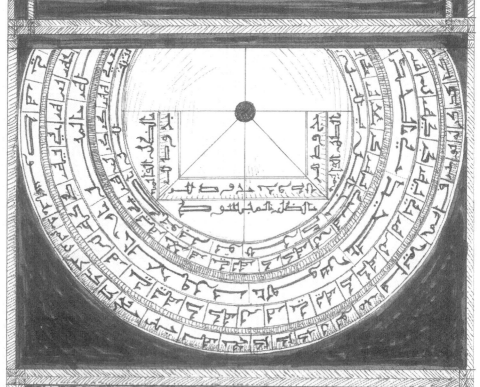

a change of seasons

By the beginning of spring 2011, scenes like this had spread across the nations of the Middle East and North Africa. A mass protest movement, starting in Tunisia, seemed to have manifested a wave of revolutions.

GAME OVER

People standing up to power.

Crowds taking to the streets in major cities, demanding human rights, democracy, economic and political reforms...

...and DIGNITY.

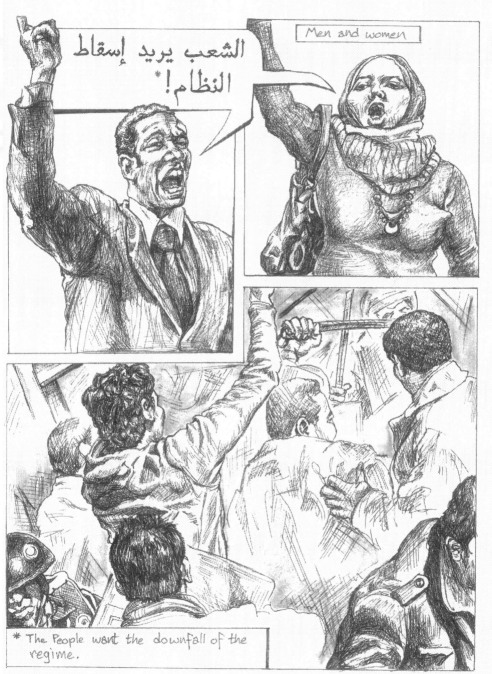

الشعب يريد إسقاط النظام!*

Men and women

* The people want the downfall of the regime.

4

Christians and Muslims together.

Egyptian Coptic Christians formed human chains around Muslim protestors while they prayed in Tahrir Square.

And Muslims stood guard outside cathedrals to prevent vandalism.

Invoking the Arab historical memory of interfaith harmony associated with the diverse society that existed in the Muslim Spanish kingdom, Al-Andalus.

6

The uprisings in Tunisia and Egypt involved mostly nonviolent protest. Thus these events were often referred to as "Jasmine" and "Lotus" revolutions, and the regional phenomenon was termed the "Arab Spring." But the floral language ignores...

...the casualties of revolution.

The martyr of Sidi Bouzid

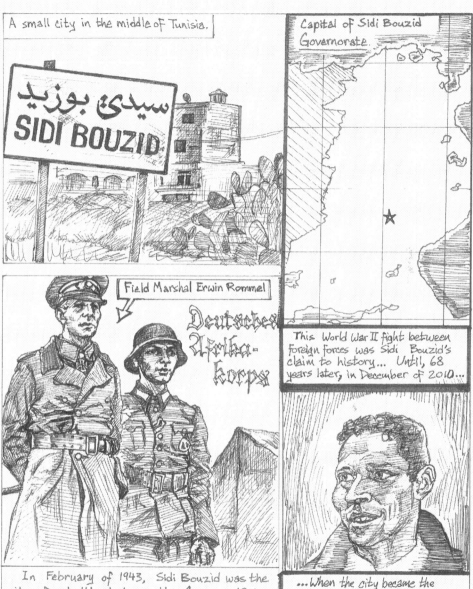

A small city in the middle of Tunisia.

SIDI BOUZID

سيدي بوزيد

Capital of Sidi Bouzid Governorate.

Field Marshal Erwin Rommel

Deutsches Afrika-Korps

This World War II fight between foreign forces was Sidi Bouzid's claim to history... Until, 68 years later, in December of 2010...

In February of 1943, Sidi Bouzid was the site of a battle between the German 10th and 21st Panzer Divisions and the United States 1st Armored Division and 168th Infantry. It was the opening of the Battle of Kasserine Pass.

...When the city became the location of a more local conflict — sparking a popular rebellion that no one thought was possible.
It began with a man named Muhammad Bouazizi.

الجمهورية التونسية
بطاقة التعريف الوطنية

09217605

اللقب بوعزيزي

الإسم طارق

بن الطيب محمد

تاريخ الولادة 29 مارس 1984

سيدي بو زيد

Tarek al-Tayyib Muhammad Bouazizi (b. March 29, 1984)

He went by 'Muhammad'

Muhammad's father died when the boy was three years old.

He and his six siblings were educated in a one-room school in the village of Sidi Saleh, twelve miles from their home in Sidi Bouzid.

His father worked in Construction in Libya.

Muhammad did not finish school.

Unemployment in Sidi Bouzid = 30%

Instead, he supported his mother, uncle, and younger siblings by selling produce in the streets.

He was known affectionately as "Basboosa".

Despite being poor, he was known to give free fruit and vegetables to families who could not afford them.

11

... He had ambitions that he never acheived. He wanted to get married and have some money to take care of his mother and Family.

He appealed to the authorities but was turned away without restitution.

FLICK

He said if no one would help him, he would burn himself alive.

Shortly afterwards he did exactly that.

Muhammad Bouazizi could not have been certain what impact his act would have... that the grief would give way...

... to something else...

There was a moment when it could have gone unreported,

One street vendor's personal frustration and desperate act of self-inflicted violence lit the fuse of a mass powder keg.

unnoticed outside of the city limits. But it WAS noticed.

He gave people the energy to speak out. The fire that inflamed Muhammad touched everybody. Every Tunisian. They understood the message that my brother wanted to deliver to the Tunisian people. *

Leila Bouazizi

Muhammad's sister

* *Problems Linger Despite Tunisian Revolution,* Nazanine Moshiri, Al Jazeera (Last Modified: 21 Apr., 2011)
<http://english.aljazeera.net/video/africa/2011/04/201142154575802207.html>

Something had changed.

BOUAZIZI

In Sidi Bouzid, and quickly across the entire country, activists, students, workers seemed to have collectively lost all fear.

17

The Protests were peaceful.

Bananas (No Weapons)

Demonstrators sat on the ground

Pledging their own blood, but determined not to shed that of others. Nonviolent Resistance.

Still, the police arrived...

Armed and ready.

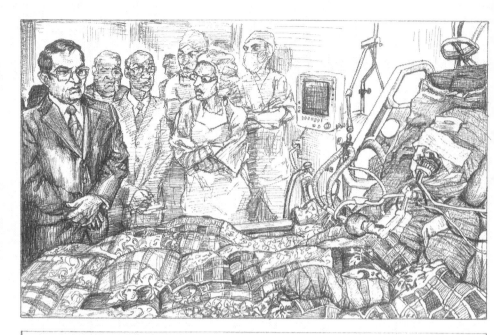

President Ben Ali visited Bouazizi in the hospital as people revolted across the country. He promised to provide the best treatment possible for the young man.

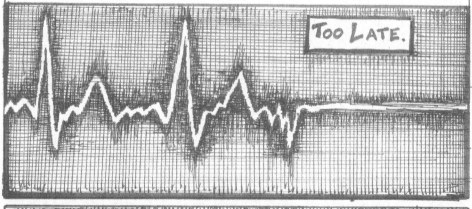

TOO LATE.

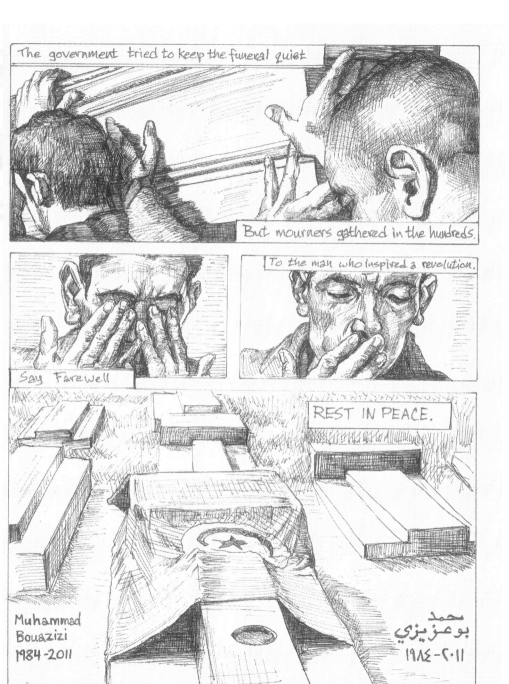

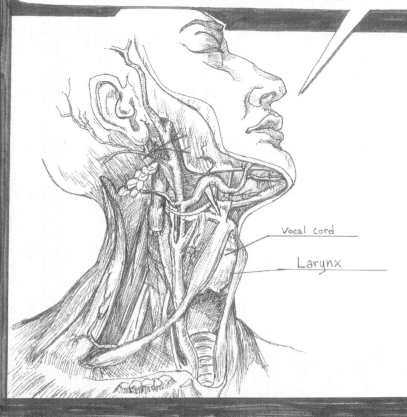

The Tunisian media avoided reporting on the unrest in Sidi Bouzid.

Breaking News: National Media Less Than Free

Meanwhile, the police tried to make sure that news-worthy disturbances ceased.

They arrived in blue vans.

Reinforced Mercedes-Benz

Tear gas gun

The government attempted to quiet the opposition with a number of statements promising reform...

We seek to develop the Tunisian economy to create jobs for these people.

...While police and military moved into the streets.

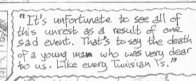

The issue of unemployment is one of concern to all parties in Tunisia. But what is NOT acceptable is for those parties to resort to violence, which is not in anyone's interest.

"It's unfortunate to see all of this unrest as a result of one sad event. That's to say the death of a young man who was very dear to us. Like every Tunisian is."

December 22

Houcine Falhi:
A 22 year-old man climbs an electrical pylon and electrocutes himself to death.
As he dies, he shouts:
"NO MISERY NO MORE UNEMPLOYMENT"

And people continued to go out in the streets.

Despite the police declaring curfews.

27

Stand back!

As civilians show their readiness to die, security forces begin to demonstrate their readiness to kill.

BANG!
BANG
BANG

28

Police fired live ammunition as well as tear gas.

Bullet Shell

December 24: At a demonstration in the town of Menzel Bouzaiene Police shoot two protestors —

44 year-old Chawki Belhoussine El Hadri.

And 18 year-old Muhammad Amari.
   Amari died, adding to the oppositions list of 'martyrs.'

The Advocate.

Déclaration Universal

Préambule

Considérant qu... la reconnaissance de la di...
de le famille hum... et de leurs droits égaux et inaliénable
fondement de ...erté, de la justice et de la paix dans le m...
considérant que la méconnaissa... et le mépris des droits de l'ho...
conduit à des actes de barbarie qu... évè... la conscie... de...
...vènement d'un monde où les êtres humains seront libres de parler et de...
...érès de le terreur et de la misère... à été proclamé...
de l'homme,
...qu'il est esse...

At night – away from cameras and crowds – police made more arrests.

The blue vans again

Open the DOOR!

Abuse by police in Tunisia is an open secret.

"Prisoners serving sentences imposed for political or security reasons are at particular risk of further abuse in prison..."

"... suspension by the ankles or in contorted positions..."

"... The most commonly reported methods of torture are beatings on the body, especially the soles of the feet..."

"... electric shocks..."

"... and burning with cigarettes..."

CLICK

"... There are also reports of mock executions..."

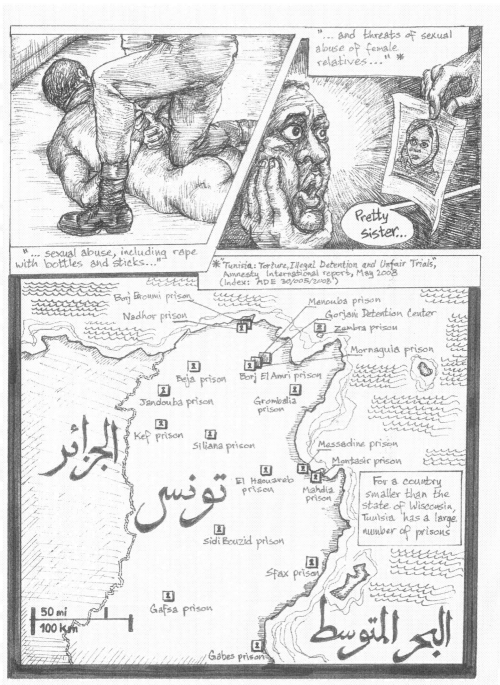

"... and threats of sexual abuse of female relatives..." *

Pretty sister...

"... sexual abuse, including rape with bottles and sticks..."

*"Tunisia: Torture, Illegal Detention and Unfair Trials", Amnesty International report, May 2008 (Index: MDE 30/005/2008)

For a country smaller than the state of Wisconsin, Tunisia has a large number of prisons

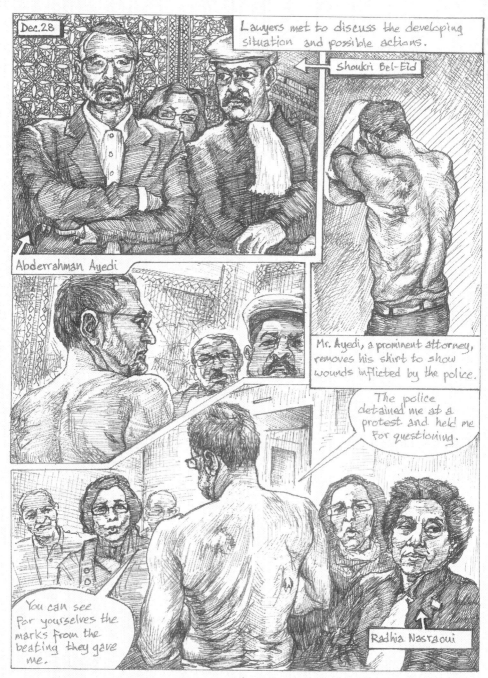

33

The lawyers resolved to assemble in protest.

إضراب زامن كرامة المحامي

They hoped that a demonstration of respectable professional litigators would add to the legitimacy of the protests.

They may also have assumed that the police would not react very harshly against this action.

They waved the national flag.

And called for reform and human rights.

راضية
نصراوي

Among the lawyers that day was Radhia Nasraoui — No stranger to police violence.

As an activist against torture and other human rights abuses in Tunisia she and her family have been subject to persistent harassment and surveillance by the government.

She was a founding member of the Association Against Torture in Tunisia (established on June 26, 2003).

Even her daughters have reportedly been stalked and intimidated by plain clothes agents of the "security forces."

Yet she has continued to denounce what she calls "systematic torture" by the Ben Ali regime.

احمد
نجيب
الشابي

The older generation opposition figures have continued legal and political efforts despite little success

◄Ahmad Najib Chebbi — Leftist activist and one of the founders of the Progressive Socialist Rally (one of Tunisia's marginalized opposition parties).

He attempted to run against Ben Ali in the 2009 election but was disqualified on technical grounds and had to withdraw.

حمه الهمامي

Radhia's husband, **Hamma Hammami**, (spokesman for the banned Communist Party of Tunisian Workers) has faced numerous charges and jail time for his political activity.

This harassment of human rights advocates and political opposition figures has been commonly reported in Tunisia.

"They are put under surveillance and have their telephone lines, Internet access and emails interrupted and often blocked... some have been physically assaulted by individuals believed to have been acting at the behest of the Tunisian security forces..."

December 28, 2007 - **Ali Ben Salem**, then 75-year-old founding member of the National Council for Liberties in Tunisia (CNLT) and the Association Against Torture in Tunisia (ALTT), was assaulted by police. He was pushed to the ground, stepped on, and his glasses were crushed.

"...Smear campaigns in the state-controlled media are organized to denigrate human rights defenders and to tarnish their reputations..."*

* "Stop Harassment of Human Rights Activists in Tunisia," June, 2010
<http://www.amnesty.org/en/appeals-for-action/stop-harassment-human-rights-activists-tunisia>

THE MASSACRE المجزرة

The violence of state forces against protesters reached new heights in Kasserine on January 7.

The intensity of clashes here and images of the resulting casualties would galvanize the Tunisian public against the regime.

Most of the shooting took place in the impoverished neighbourhood of Ezzouhour.

The city of Kasserine (Qasrayn) - at the foot of Tunisia's tallest peak - Jebel ech-Chambi.

Student protests had begun to grow in strength and regularity after school resumed on January 3.

Local police had a limited response, doing little to disperse the demonstrations.

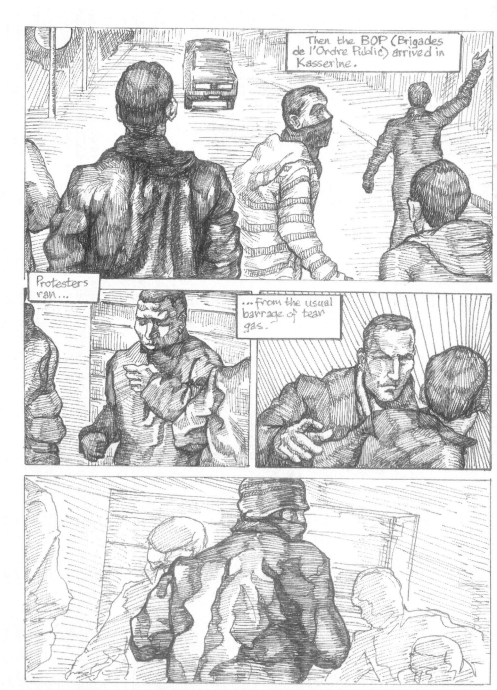

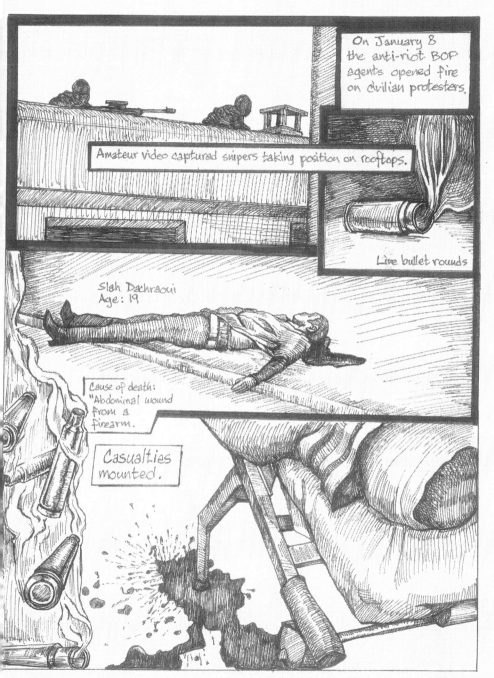

On January 8 the anti-riot BOP agents opened fire on civilian protesters.

Amateur video captured snipers taking position on rooftops.

Live bullet rounds

Slah Dachraoui
Age: 19

Cause of death: "Abdominal wound from a firearm.

Casualties mounted.

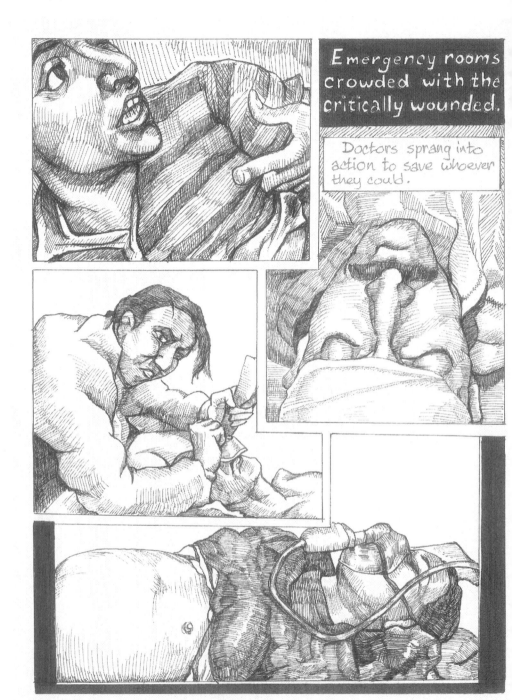

Emergency rooms crowded with the critically wounded.

Doctors sprang into action to save whoever they could.

Hospital waiting rooms filled with those less intensely injured...

Concerned family and friends ...

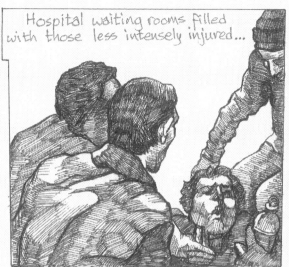

The bereaved.

The only silence was with those beyond help.

44

The next day, January 19, 2011

Business as usual at the women's hammam* on Monguela roundabout.

Women of all ages

As well as children

* The hammam is a traditional public sauna.

Four agents in black uniforms and masks arrived.

6230 RIOT CS SMOKE

They shot teargas into the hammam.

45

46

Among the semi-clothed women fleeing the hammam was Monia Omri along with her young daughter.

One of the agents chased after them, yelling and cussing.

Twenty-three-year-old Saber Rtibi was coming out of a grocery store when he saw his neighbour, Monia, being pursued down the street.

When Rtibi tried to protect his neighbour the pursuing agent shot him in the belly.

Witnesses say the agent then removed her helmet and shook her long blond hair.

And blew kisses at the man she shot.

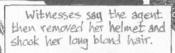

Saber Rtibi was about to move to France with his father.

Instead he died slowly of a bullet wound to the belly.

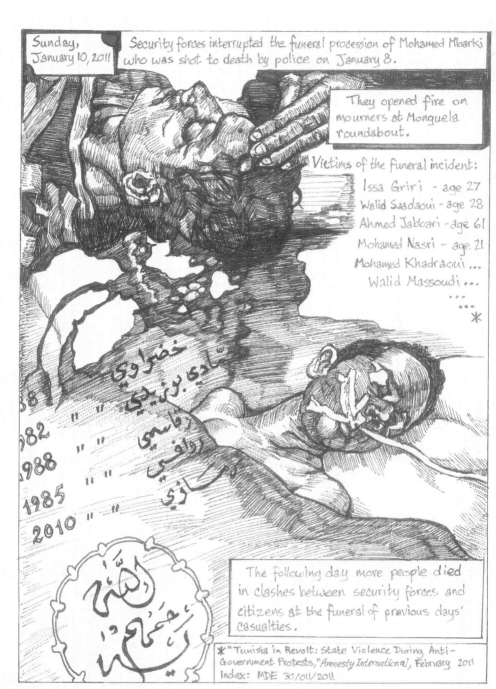

Sunday, January 10, 2011

Security forces interrupted the funeral procession of Mohamed Mbarki who was shot to death by police on January 8.

They opened fire on mourners at Monquela roundabout.

Victims of the funeral incident:

Issa Griri - age 27
Walid Saadaoui - age 28
Ahmed Jabloari - age 61
Mohamed Nasri - age 21
Mohamed Khadraoui ...
Walid Massoudi ...
...
*

The following day more people died in clashes between security forces and citizens at the funeral of previous days' casualties.

*"Tunisia in Revolt: State Violence During Anti-Government Protests," Amnesty International, February 2011 Index: MDE 30/011/2011

49

Similar incidents of police violence, including the use of live ammunition were reported in Thala and Rgeb.

Angry civilians burned government offices and banks...

... Hurled improvised gas bombs at police...

... And created smoke screens by burning tires.

Snipers in Kasserine and Thala used expanding or "Dum-dum" bullets designed either with a hollow or soft point.

They are especially damaging because they expand and break up on impact, creating a larger-diameter wound.

The Hague Convention prohibits the use of expanding bullets in war:
"The Contracting Parties agree to abstain from the use of bullets which expand or flatten easily in the human body…"
— Hague IV, Declaration III – Concerning the Prohibition of the Use of Expanding Bullets, July 29, 1899 26 Martens Nouveau Recueil (ser.2)1002, 187 Consol. T.S. 459, entered into force September 4, 1900

The identity of the snipers has yet to be ascertained but it has been conjectured that they were an elite unit not attached to the regular police nor the BOP.

52

PATER·PATRIAE

FATHER OF THE NATION

زعيم الأمة

He studied at Special Inter-service in Saint-Cyr ...

... and the artillery school in Chalons-Sur-Marne in France.

As well as the Senior Intelligence School in Maryland,

and the School of Anti-Aircraft Field Artillery in Texas, USA.

After 16 years in active military service he served briefly as Ambassador to Poland.

Then as Minister of state and Interior Minister before he ascended to the post of Prime Minister in 1986.

On November 7, 1987, President Habib Bourguiba was declared medically incapable of fulfilling his duties. In conformity with Article 57 of the Tunisian constitution, Ben Ali took over the presidency.

President Bourguiba –

الفصل ٥٧

عند شغور منصب رئيس الجمهورية لوفاة أو لعجز قام يتولى فورا رئيس مجلس أمام مكتب المجلس

This peaceful coup d'état renewed hope that democracy would develop in Tunisia under the guidance of Ben Ali. But Bourguiba had not always been considered an obstacle to freedom.

Ben Ali was twenty years old when his country won its independence from France in 1956

Guerrilla Fighters

Tunisian Nationalist

Future President Habib Bourguiba in Bizerte, 1952

As with all Decolonizations of the 20th century, Tunisia did not achieve this without struggle...

European powers had agreed that France would take over Tunisia at the Congress of Berlin in 1878.

The Ottoman Empire, of which Tunisia was a part at the time, had just been defeated in a war with Russia. Territorial concessions ensued.

On April 28th, 1881, 28 thousand French troops invaded Tunisia ...

Establishing a French occupation that would last until the middle of the 20th century.

HABIB BOURGUIBA
حبيب بورقيبة
1903 - 2000

Resistance to French colonization grew in the 1930s. Habib Bourguiba became a prominent resistance figure. He had studied Law and Political Science in Paris and became active in the Destour Party when he returned to Tunisia in the late 1920s.

Photos of a young Bourguiba upon arrest by French forces.

Following a split with the party mainstream in 1934, Bourguiba and other prominent nationalists formed the Neo Destour Party at Ksar Hellal on March 2, 1934.

Bourguiba's anti-colonial activism caught the attention of the French authorities who confined him to Bourj-Leboeuf prison in September, 1934.

BORDJ LEBŒUF — Dépôt C¹ᵉ Saharienne

As a revolutionary, Bourguiba was intent on gaining Tunisian independence. Still, he never wanted to be an enemy of the former colonial masters. During World War II, when Axis forces freed him from prison and tried to gain native allegiance in North Africa, Bourguiba declared his support for the Allied Powers.

On March 20, 1956, Tunisia gained independence from France with Habib Bourguiba as its first President.

President Habib Bourguiba

After Independence the French military maintained control over the strategic port city of Bizerte.

France had promised to negotiate the removal of their base but in fact planned to expand it.

In 1961 Tunisian forces blockaded the French naval base.

Charles de Gaulle, President of the French 5th Republic. (1959-1969)

Le Vile de Bizerte, 1961

The French responded by sending 800 Paratroopers in reinforcement.

Tunisian forces opened fire on the French paratroopers.

France then launched a full scale invasion of the town of Bizerte. After heavy street fighting the French still held on to the port. They did not relinquish control of Bizerte until 1963.

Despite this violent incident Bourguiba sustained good relations with France throughout his rule.

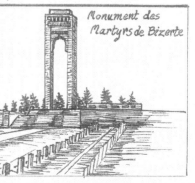
Monument des Martyrs de Bizerte

58

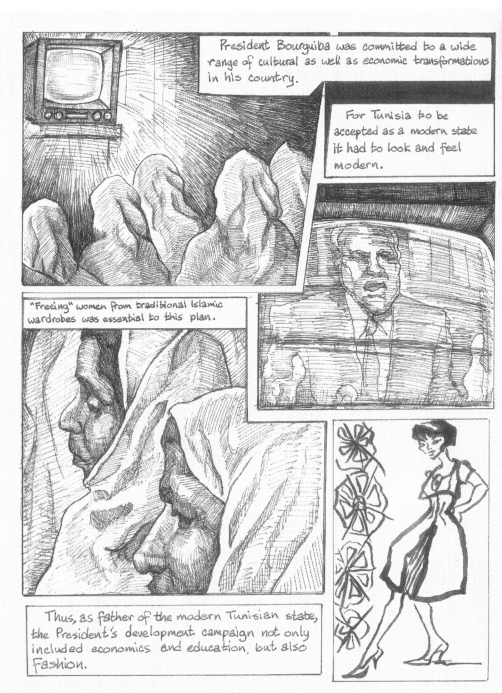

President Bourguiba was committed to a wide range of cultural as well as economic transformations in his country.

For Tunisia to be accepted as a modern state it had to look and feel modern.

"Freeing" women from traditional Islamic wardrobes was essential to this plan.

Thus, as father of the modern Tunisian state, the President's development campaign not only included economics and education, but also Fashion.

The presidential motorcade toured the cities and villages of the "New" Tunisia.

An indigenous "Mission Civilisatrice."

Promoting his social agenda of modernization.

Robe en mousseline noire plissée soleil de Blanchini Férie Chapeau Heln

فستان من الموسلين الأسود
« البليسي »
قماش « بيكيني فيريي »
قبعة « هالن »

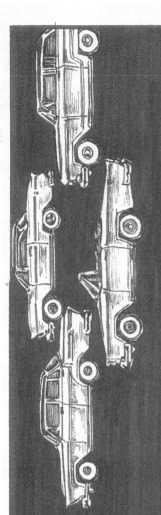

PROGRESS

and

DEVELOPMENT!

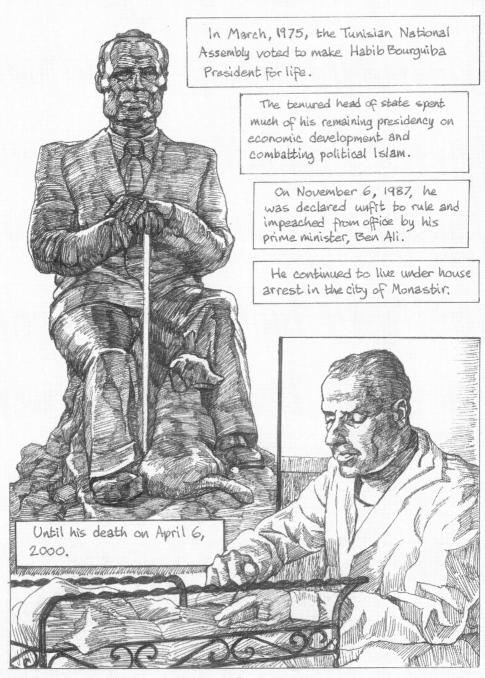

In March, 1975, the Tunisian National Assembly voted to make Habib Bourguiba President for life.

The tenured head of state spent much of his remaining presidency on economic development and combatting political Islam.

On November 6, 1987, he was declared unfit to rule and impeached from office by his prime minister, Ben Ali.

He continued to live under house arrest in the city of Monastir.

Until his death on April 6, 2000.

Ben Ali promised reform and democracy.

What he delivered was an increasingly draconian one-party police state.

The major target of state repression was political Islam.

"More than 10,000 Islamists and other opponents went to Ben Ali's prisons in the 1990s." *

But even after Islamist politics receded from electoral and social relevance in Tunisia, the government's iron fist did not soften.

The man who would be democrat became indistinguishable from a King.

* "The Rise and Fall of Ben Ali," Christopher Alexander, in Revolution in the Arab World: Tunisia, Egypt and the Unmaking of An Era, Ed. Marc Lynch, Susan B. Glesser, Blake Hounshell

Political freedom was not the only promise broken by the Tunisian government. Economic expectations also changed.

Tunisia's command economy was based on a bargain by which the state provided benefits to the population in exchange for obedience.

It used to be that subsidies were middle class welfare. ... it was across the board.

This economic arrangement collapsed in the last decades of the 20th century, largely encouraged by international advisors.

The IMF [International Monetary Fund] basically said, "You can't do that"... You can only subsidize for... "absolute poverty," as they call it.

So what they began to do is remove subsidies from a varity of consumer items...

Eventually what of course happened was people were extraordinarily angry... not just because food was going to cost them more, but because the state was violating the contract — the social compact — which is: "Sit down, shut up, and we'll take care of you."

...There's no reason for the people to sit down and shut up anymore if the state wasn't going to take care of them.

Prof. James Gelvin – UCLA

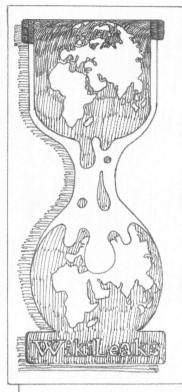

In December 2010, WikiLeaks published a document from the US embassy in Tunis written in June, 2008

The author of the report was American ambassador Robert F. Godec.

"According to Transparency International's annual survey and Embassy contacts' observations, corruption in Tunisia is getting worse..."

"President Ben Ali's extended family is often cited as the nexus of Tunisian corruption."

"The numerous stories of familial corruption are certainly galling to many Tunisians, but beyond the rumors of money-grabbing is a frustration that the well-connected can live outside the law."

"This government has based its legitimacy on its ability to deliver economic growth, but a growing number of Tunisians believe those at the top are keeping the benefits for themselves."

"Corruption is a problem that is at once both political and economic. The lack of transparency and accountability that characterize Tunisia's political system similarly plague the economy, damaging the investment climate and fueling a culture of corruption. For all the talk of a Tunisian economic miracle and all the positive statistics, the fact that Tunisia's own investors are steering clear speaks volumes. Corruption is the elephant in the room; it is the problem everyone knows about, but no one can publicly acknowledge."

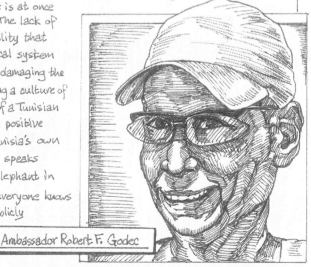

Ambassador Robert F. Godec

The Ben Alis

"Often referred to as a quasi-mafia, an oblique mention of 'the Family' is enough to indicate which family you mean."

"In 2006, Imad and Moaz Trabelsi, Ben Ali's nephews, are reported to have stolen the yacht of a well-connected French businessman... The theft, widely reported in the French press, came to light when the yacht, freshly painted to cover distinguishing characteristics, appeared in the Sidi Bou Said harbor."

Ben Ali's speech came a little too late. It was becoming increasingly clear that — after 24 years in office — the president had become the major focus of popular outrage.

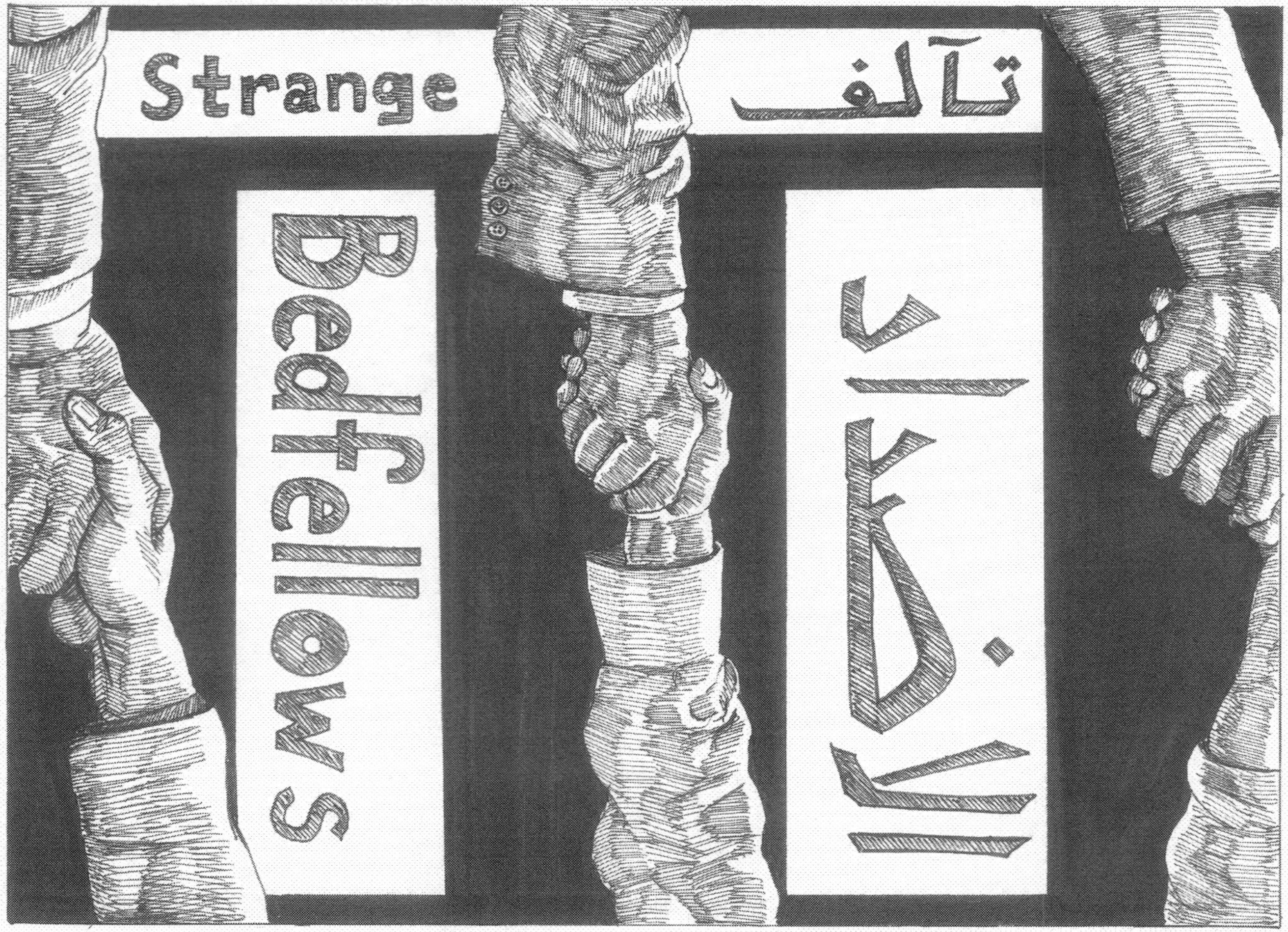
Strange
Bedfellows
تآلف
الاضداد

The opposition could have been the source of a few jokes too:

An Islamist, a communist, a worker and a student go to a protest...

A popular crack had it that even the president's hairdresser had joined the protests.

The major Tunisian religious opposition group: Al-Nahda (The Renaissance)

النَّهْضَة

As with most Islamist movements, Al-Nahda traces its intellectual geneology thinkers like Sayyid Qutb,

The Egyptian Muslim revivalist and ideological influence on the Muslim Brotherhood, who was executed for his beliefs in 1966.

In the 1980s Tunisian Islamists moved towards acceptance of popular sovereignty and the democratic process.

They claimed to be developing a new form of "Tunisian Islam."

And Maulana Maududi, the founder of Jamaat-e-Islami

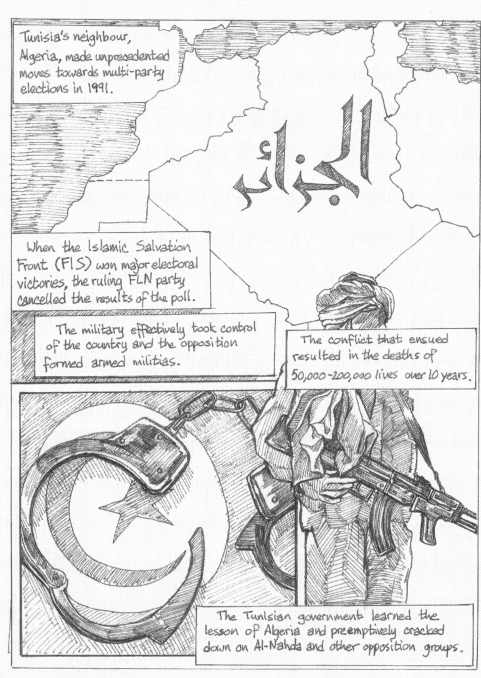

Tunisia's neighbour, Algeria, made unprecedented moves towards multi-party elections in 1991.

الجزائر

When the Islamic Salvation Front (FIS) won major electoral victories, the ruling FLN party cancelled the results of the poll.

The military effectively took control of the country and the opposition formed armed militias.

The conflict that ensued resulted in the deaths of 50,000-200,000 lives over 10 years.

The Tunisian government learned the lesson of Algeria and preemptively cracked down on Al-Nahda and other opposition groups.

January 2, 2011

▫ The Tunisian uprising gains support from an unlikely corner

▫ The cyber activist network, "Anonymous," announces: OPERATION TUNISIA

Anonymous was born on IRC (Internet Chat Relay) channels like 4chan.org

IRC was created by Jarkko Oikarinen (AKA WIZ) in 1988

ANONYMOUS

/b/ - Random:

A section of the imageboard, 4chan, devoted to nothing in particular.

In the image board sub culture, "channers," communicating with the screen name "anonymous," exchange erotica, offensive slurs, obscenities, and absurd laughs ("lullz"). On this virtual playground the only thing held sacred is internet freedom.

File: 130596614.jpg - (70 KB 209×187)

☐ Anonymous 05/27/11 (Fri) 3:47:46 No. 33078 [Reply]

The channer's cultural currency is the "meme" - an image, video, web address, joke, etc. that is spread across chat and image boards and social media.

Humorous images of cats are staple memes, as are nude images of women.

I CAN HAS CHEEZBURGER?

77

The anonymous channers developed a political identity and cause in circumstances that were appropriately strange.

We are the authorities on getting people off drugs, we are the authorities on the mind, we are the authorities on improving conditions...

When, in 2008, the Church of Scientology removed an unauthorized clip of an interview with actor Tom Cruise (discussing the virtues of his new age faith) from internet circulation for copyright reasons, the channers found a natural enemy.

"Anonymous" became the non-identity behind a cyber attack campaign.

They released a statement – a time-lapsed video of cityscapes with an electronic voice-over, addressing the institution of Scientology.

☐ Over the years we have been watching you. Your campaigns of misinformation. Your suppression of dissent. Your litigious nature. All of these things have caught our eye. We shall proceed to expel you from the internet and systematically dismantle the church of Scientology in its present form...

WE ARE ANONYMOUS
WE ARE LEGION
WE DO NOT FORGIVE
WE DO NOT FORGET
EXPECT US.

The collective "hive mind" of the anonymous internet activists (the "anons") unleashed a cyber assault on their declared enemy, taking down the Scientology website with a distributed denial of service (DDoS) attack.

OPERATION CHANOLOGY

ANONYMOUS WANTS YOU

TO GET YOUR ASS BEHIND A PROXY AND JOIN THE RAID

Anonymous — without a political program beyond an anarchic mantra of freedom — engaged in a number of absurdist and even cruel acts of annoyance and sabotage against seemingly arbitrary targets (including the Epilepsy Foundation of America).

But in 2009, when protests broke out in Iran over allegations of vote rigging, Anonymous provided web resources to by-pass Iranian government censorship.

Then what seemed like a fleeting internet rage became concrete as anons staged actual live protest events.

They wore Guy Faukes masks, inspired by Alan Moore's *V for Vendetta*.

Click Here To Help Iran

With "Operation Leakspin," the anons came to the defense of Wikileaks and its editor in chief, Julian Assange.

And in 2011, Anonymous launched "Operation Tunisia" in solidarity with pro-democracy protests, hacking Tunisian government websites.

January 6, 2011: 21 year-old rapper, Hamada Ben Amor (AKA El Général) was arrested for the political content of his lyrics.

El Général had generated a buzz with a music video distributed online for his rap song, "Rais El-Bled" (Head of State) in which he verbally confronts the president.

The video opens with old footage of President Ben Ali talking to school children.

Then El Général takes the mic.

Mr. President, I speak to you today in the name
Of everyone in 2011 living in pain
Un heard voices of those people who die
When all they really want is to work to get by...

After news of the death toll in Kasserine and Thala spread, marches and demonstrations multiplied, expanding to include all demographics. The youth movement became a nationwide rebellion.

But with the enormous masses on the streets of the nation

And the arrival of the international press, police were under increased pressure to avoid abuses of human rights

• Local Tunisian broadcasting was regulated by the Tunisian Radio and Television Establishment (ERTT) - a state-run agency.

• Satellite channels side-stepped state controls on media. Al-Jazeera (based in Qatar) was among the first satellite news outlets to report on the situation from the ground.

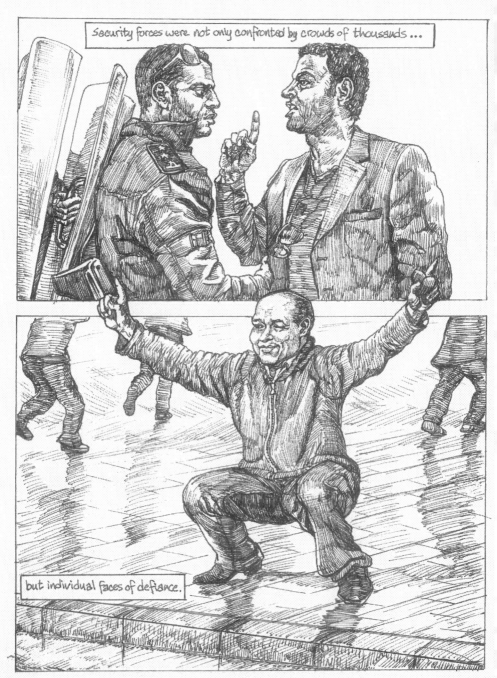

Faces of revolution.

The army still refused to use force against civilians.

The people responded with welcoming cheers and bouquets of flowers.

As clashes spread, police abandoned their regular duties, leaving private property vulnerable to opportunistic looters and thieves.

Civilians filled the void left by absent law enforcement by creating neighbourhood defense committees.

Armed with whatever they had available, they set up checkpoints and guard posts.

Labor unions announced general strikes.

Bringing the economy to a standstill

And making workers available to go to the streets.

Thursday, January 13 - Ben Ali met with Abdelssalam Jrad, head of Tunisia's General labor union.

That night the President addressed the nation for what would be the last time.

In the name of God, the beneficent, the merciful. People of Tunisia, I speak to you today, all of you, in Tunisia and abroad, in the language of all Tunisians. I speak to you now because the situation dictates deep changes. Deep and comprehensive. And I have understood you all - the unemployed, the needy, the political, and those calling for more freedoms. I have understood you all. But the events taking place in our country today... are not part of our tradition...

Destruction is not part of Tunisian tradition... And the unrest must stop... We must all make an effort to end it, together... hand in hand, for the sake of our country.

My pain and sorrow are great. I have spent more than fifty years of my life in the service of Tunisia, in various capacities... And I have made countless sacrifices and I never accept - you all know - I cannot accept the shedding of a single drop of Tunisian blood.

Prime Minister Mohammed Ghannouchi made a brief appearance on state television:

In the name of God, the beneficent, the merciful. Fellow citizens, in accordance with the provisions of the Constitution — which stipulates that, should the President of the Republic be temporarily unable to carry out his duties, his powers will be delegated to the Prime Minister — and in view of the fact that the President is temporarily unable to exercise his duties and functions,

I hereby, effective immediately, assume the duties and powers of the President of the Republic.

I call on all sons and daughters of Tunisia, from all political and intellectual affiliations, and from all classes and denominations...

... to adhere to the spirit of patriotism and unity in order to enable our country — which is dear to all of us — to make it through this difficult phase, and to regain its security and its stability. And I pledge during this period of my assuming this responsibility to honor the Constitution, and undertake the political, economic and social reforms which have been announced. And to do this very meticulously and in dialogue with different national sides of parties and national organizations...

15

إذا الشعب يوما أراد الحياة

فلا بد أن يستجيب القدر !

"If, one day, a people desires to Live,
Then, fate will answer their call!" *

* From the famous poem, "If the People on Day Desire Life,"
by Abu al-Qasim al-Shabi, Translation by Elliot Colla

After the proud celebrations of victory, following Ben Ali's departure, the question still remained: where is Tunisia heading?

The events of December 2010 and January 2011 were momentous. Still, the corruption, inequality and poverty that brought people out to the streets would not disappear over night.

This is not the end. It is only a beginning.

ACKNOWLEDGEMENTS

The author would like to thank Prof. James Gelvin, Prof. Douja Mamelouk, Prof. Saree Makdisi, and Bechir Blagui for their input and encouragement on this book. He must also express thanks to the following friends and mentors: Meg Biddle, Marcia Perry, Jim Dultz, Goleen Samari, the Kodl family, his parents, brothers, and everyone else who has supported him.

KHALID HUSSEN was born in 1985 in Saudi Arabia to an Egyptian Father and an American mother. He received an informal education throughout his childhood, which was spent between the United States and the Middle East. He received a BA in Studio Art and MA in Islamic Studies from UCLA.

Khalid Hussein lives and works in Los Angeles, CA.

Made in the USA
San Bernardino, CA
16 June 2019